PACIFIC NO

Published by Gallery Books
A Division of W H Smith Publishers Inc.
112 Madison Avenue
New York, New York 10016

Produced by
Bison Books Corp.
15 Sherwood Place
Greenwich, CT 06830

ISBN 0-8317-6714-6

Printed in Hong Kong

2 3 4 5 6 7 8 9 10

INTRODUCTION

A land of majestic beauty and astonishing diversity is summoned up by the phrase 'Pacific Northwest.' The mind's eye is drawn to the rugged coast that runs north from Cape Mendocino, California, to the Olympic Peninsula of Washington State. Here, wind-swept beaches broken by rocky promontories yield to dense coniferous forests that recede to the omnipresent mountains. The lonely coastal highway can be glimpsed only rarely from a vantage point offshore, threading its way along the woodlands.

It is no accident that the cities of the Pacific Northwest were not built along this coast, but farther inland, where sheltered harbors on the Columbia River system and arms of the Pacific offer a more hospitable environment for man and his works. From prosperous Portland, Oregon, near the mouth of the Columbia, to youthful Anchorage, Alaska, on sheltered Cook Inlet, Northwestern cities are closely tied to navigable waterways that have carried people and goods through the region since Indian times. Seattle and Olympia, Washington, grew up around the great inland sea of Puget Sound and the inlets north of it. These give access to British Columbia's beautiful island city of Victoria; 40 miles north, across the Strait of Georgia, is Vancouver, Canada's third largest city and a treasure house of natural and man-made attractions. Ships based in Vancouver and other nearby ports make the Inside Passage through the grandeur of Coastal Alaska. These inland waterways are alive with ferries, steamships, tugs, fishing boats and private craft of every kind.

Islands are another prominent feature of this land. The San Juan group in the Strait of Juan de Fuca, between the Pacific and Puget Sound, includes 172 islands—a major unspoiled recreational area for the region's people. Just north of here, British Columbia's Gulf Islands number more than a hundred, widely scattered between Vancouver Island and the mainland. Lumbering, fishing, and other water-related industries are still important here, as they have been since pioneer days.

The coastal region is divided by the Cascade Range from a very different land that rolls east to the Rocky Mountains. The Cascades are volcanic peaks crowned by ice and snow, marching from British Columbia south into northern California. They comprise a world of their own, in which sudden peaks shoulder up over wildflower meadows, and waterfalls plummet hundreds of feet into deep gorges rimmed by virgin forest. Three national parks protect vast tracts of this unique wilderness, from Washington's North Cascades and the environs of Mount Rainier to Oregon's Crater Lake, a blue jewel embedded in the broken crown of an ancient volcano. The twentieth century has seen several volcanic eruptions in this long- quiescent range, including that of Novarupta, on Alaska's Katmai Peninsula, and Mount St Helens in Washington.

Moisture-laden clouds from the Pacific drop most of their rainfall west of the natural barrier formed by the Cascades. Thus Washington's Olympic Peninsula has the greatest temperate-zone rain forests in the hemisphere, and Douglas fir predominates in the coastal forests. East of the Cascades, Ponderosa pine takes over, and the forests become more scattered,

For Roni and Louis

3-6 Seattle at twilight, with Mount Rainier in the background.

RTHWEST

| TEXT | ROBIN LANGLEY SOMMER |
| DESIGN | MIKE ROSE |

GALLERY BOOKS
An imprint of W.H. Smith Publishers Inc.
112 Madison Avenue
New York, New York 10016

A Bison Book

interspersed with meadows. The eastern foothills gradually give way to the wonders of the Columbia River Basin, where torrential streams have cut deep gorges through a landscape formed by lava and ice flows millennia ago. What could have been a desert area due to the relatively sparse rainfall between the Cascades and the Rockies is a fertile agricultural region boasting orchards, grain fields and cattle ranches. Grand Coulee Dam, astride the mighty Columbia River, testifies to man's part in fulfilling the promise of this land.

North of Washington lies the rich province of British Columbia, Canada's gateway to the Pacific and the Orient. British Columbia prides itself on its natural beauties and has developed a lifestyle equally attuned to land and sea—Vancouver's ferry system is the most extensive in the world. The coastal cities of Victoria and Vancouver offer every amenity, from a diverse cultural life to an international cuisine. These urban centers enjoy a natural setting unmatched almost anywhere else—over 350,000 square miles of rugged and beautiful country.

British Columbia's northern boundary is America's largest state. In Alaska and the Yukon, too, man has had a sometimes stormy but always vital relationship with nature. Coastal Alaska is a microcosm of all that this great region can call its own: soaring mountains, massive glaciers, abundant fish and wildlife, far-flung archipelagos and an energetic people who combine an Indian, Russian and pioneer heritage.

The native peoples of the Pacific Northwest were fishermen and gatherers, who found ample food in their waters and woods. They caught salmon and halibut, gathered roots and berries, hunted whales and elk. Many place names recall the original inhabitants of this region, from Seattle, named for Chief Sealth, who befriended early pioneers, to British Columbia's Nootka Sound.

Other Northwestern place names hark back to the early European and American explorers who sought the legendary Northwest Passage through the continent—men like Captain James Cook, who put in at what is now Vancouver Island in 1778, and Robert Gray, who named the Columbia River for his flagship in 1792.

After Lewis and Clark made their overland expedition to the mouth of the Columbia River (1805-06), fur traders and trappers flocked into the Northwest, closely followed by settlers and missionaries. In Alaska, Russian settlements grounded in the fur trade had proliferated since the eighteenth century. British Columbian trappers and settlers competed hotly for their share of the valuable pelts, first under auspices of the North West Company, then under the powerful Hudson's Bay Company. In 1856 there were fewer than 800 colonists in the Canadian territory. Then the discovery of gold on the Fraser River (1858) brought a major influx of settlers—some 30,000 in a single year. Twenty years later, the gold rush hit Alaska and the Yukon, soon after the United States had purchased them from Russia (to the dismay of critics in Congress, who called the territory 'that great lump of ice').

London and Washington reached agreement over disputed territory in the

Northwest in 1846, when the 49th parallel, from the Rockies to the Pacific, became the boundary between US and British holdings. South of this line, towns and farms had been springing up along the Willamette River, in what is now Oregon, since the early 1800s. Oregon Territory settlers soon crossed the Columbia to build up the area around Puget Sound. By 1851 Olympia, the future capital of Washington State, was a thriving village; a settlement at Alki Point would burgeon into space-age Seattle within a hundred years.

The vitality of the Northwestern pioneers can still be felt today, as the region's diverse attractions draw more and more residents and visitors. Far-seeing conservation policies have preserved the wilderness heritage, while making it accessible to those in search of both active recreation and unhurried communion with nature. Ski slopes are within hailing distance of major cities; camping, climbing, and boating are pursued avidly; naturalists of every kind can range from the changeful tide pools of the Pacific shoreline to the waterfalls of the Columbia River Basin.

Those who make their homes in the Northwest are hard to transplant: their roots are sunk deeply into its soil, whether native or adopted, and they flourish here as nowhere else. Their attachment to the land is seen in prosperous farms, tranquil fishing villages, bustling seaports and waterways, and secluded retreats. This last frontier of North America still exerts its mysterious attraction, even on those who have never been here. Jack London described it as 'the call of the wild,' and those who respond to it have found their place in the world.

THE NORTHERN PACIFIC COAST

If one were to sail from Puget Sound to Cape Mendocino, California, he would enjoy a unique perspective of the rugged Northwest Coast as the early explorers saw it. The shoreline has changed little, despite the great migration to the West of the last two centuries. Indians still live here, and the occasional fishing port or village blends harmoniously into its wooded backdrop.

In the calm waters of Puget Sound, numerous islands of every size offer anchorage, campsites and picnic grounds, but once into the Pacific, the wind travels with the force of its long sweep across the ocean. From the Olympic Peninsula south, rocky headlands and outcroppings thrust into the surf, which is sometimes thunderous and battering, sometimes tranquil. Silvered driftwood cast up by winter storms is scattered among the kelp-strewn dunes, and tide pools are alive with colorful anemones, starfish, crabs and sea urchins.

The Columbia River, the Northwest's major waterway, flows into the Pacific near Astoria, Oregon, where John Jacob Astor sought to build a fur-trading empire. Trappers, traders and settlers all used this great river, the Mississippi of the West, as their principal route through the Cascades. Early explorers mistook it for the fabled Northwest Passage, for which mariners of many lands had searched.

All the way down the coast, the distant mountains are clothed in fir and spruce, then in redwood, signaling the approach to northern California. The overland route along the coastal highway gives a nearer view of the great stands of timber still flourishing in this region. From any vantage point, it is easy to see why this land beckoned so strongly to the explorers and settlers who came here. Its rare natural beauty is matched by the richness of its resources—water, fish, game, plant life, furs and minerals. The native inhabitants were friendly to newcomers, and numerous tributaries of the Columbia offered access to the interior all the way to Idaho. What began as sparse and tenuous settlements would soon grow into dynamic cities, built upon lumber, fishing and agriculture.

Although the region has gained steadily in population and industry for over a hundred years, the Northwest Coast shows few signs of man's conquest. Vast stretches remain wilderness areas; many are protected as such for posterity. People resort here mainly for the unbroken peace of the land and seascapes, or to test their powers against the forces of nature—wind, weather and tide.

15 Cape Disappointment, Washington, where Canby Light warns mariners of the perilous Columbia River Bar. The cape takes its name from the many shipwrecks that have occurred here.

16-17 Oregon's coastal dunes, continually resculpted by Pacific storms and tides, are a study in natural beauty.

18-19 A deserted beach on the Oregon coast offers an almost lunar landscape for the solitary visitor enthralled by the sea.

20 California poppies brighten the shoreline north of Cape Mendocino.

21 Cape Flattery, on Washington's northwest coast, was named by Captain James Cook, who recorded that he was flattered by the false hope of a safe harbor there.

22-23 Haystack Rock at Cannon Beach, Oregon, where 'sea stacks' eroded into grotesque or fanciful shapes command the shoreline. The Cannon/Crescent Beach area is part of Ecola State Park.

24 Many sailors have come to grief in the turbulent waters off the Northwest Coast.

25 Arch Rock, crowned by a few hardy hemlocks, off the Curry County shoreline, Oregon.

26 Northwesterners take to the water like otters: it plays a major part in their recreational life.

27 Hopeful clam diggers fan out across Bandon Beach, Oregon, on a May morning at Coquille Point.

28-29 Sea stacks brood over the Oregon coast in the last light of day.

30 The Carson Mansion, an exceptional example of the popular nineteenth-century 'carpenter's Gothic' style—Eureka, California.

31 Restful havens like the St Orris Inn in northern California have been a feature of the Northwest Coast for over a century.

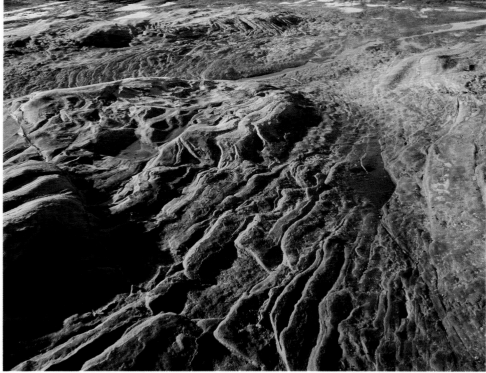

32 above *East of California's Coast Range, the land becomes much drier as a result of lesser rainfall.*

32 below *Ebb tide reveals the age-old geological strata underlying the shoreline.*

33 *The 300-foot coast redwood, king of trees, dominates the coast of northern California. Its Latin name, sempervirens, means ever-living: some specimens are 2000 years old.*

34-35 *A lighthouse stands sentinel over the coast of Oregon.*

THE OLYMPIC PENINSULA AND PUGET SOUND

Roughly half of the Olympic Peninsula, Washington's northwestern corner, is given over to national park and forest land. The focal point of this beautiful wilderness area is snow-crowned Mount Olympus, aptly named for the ancient home of the gods. Graceful mountain goats spurn the force of gravity on its steepest slopes, which challenge experienced climbers and skiers. West of the mountains, dense forests press to the coastline, and elk, deer, and bear roam freely. In this wettest section of the country, lush rain forests with Douglas firs over 200 feet tall are the most extensive on the continent.

Along the Olympic Highway, which circles the Peninsula, are the towns, villages and resort communities of the region. Many residents are born outdoorsmen, who have ready access to the fishing streams and lakes, campgrounds and trails that are so plentiful here. The state capital, Olympia, lies between the Olympic Mountains and Mount Rainier, which has the largest single-peak glacier system in the United States outside of Alaska. Shipping and lumber built Olympia, but its primary business now is government, and the gracious State Capitol complex with its rhododendron and rose gardens in bloom, is one of the city's major attractions.

Puget Sound, adjacent to the peninsula, is a fully navigable arm of the Pacific that has played a vital role in the development of the Northwest. Seattle, on Elliott Bay, is a major seaport despite the fact that it is over 100 miles from the open ocean. The city's flourishing economy owes much to the aerospace and maritime industries, and its friendly people are eager to acquaint visitors with the beauties of Seattle Center—the 1962 World's Fairgrounds—and nearby Mount Rainier National Park. Boating is so popular on Puget Sound, with its 1800 miles of bays and inlets, that the area has more pleasure boats per person than any other part of the West. Seattle's annual Seafair is a major regional event.

Reminiscent of San Francisco, which enjoys a comparable natural setting, Seattle's streets climb uphill from the waterfront, and delightful city parks provide frequent oases from the noise of commerce and industry. The city's unique Waterfront Park, built out over Elliott Bay on pilings, offers a panoramic view of the numerous ferry boats, fishing craft and other swift or stately ships making their daily rounds on this inland sea. In this water-oriented world, one can depart almost on impulse for points north: the unspoiled San Juan Islands, the rugged coast of British Columbia and the Inside Passage through Alaskan waters.

37 A ferryboat plies the peaceful waters of Puget Sound at dusk.

38-39 Mukkaw Bay on Washington's Olympic Peninsula: the native Makah Indians still live here.

40-41 Seattle, Washington, on Puget Sound—a vital city built on maritime commerce that has led the region into the aerospace age.

42 A boat parade on Seattle's popular Lake Washington, where hydroplane races climax the city's annual Seafair.

43 Elegant yachts at Shilshole Bay Marina, as seen from Sunset Hill, site of one of Seattle's numerous public parks and gardens.

44 Mount Rainier National Park is Washington's most frequented recreation center for skiing, camping, hiking and climbing.

45 Colorful costumes are part of Seattle's week-long Seafair, held at midsummer. A Grand Parade leads off the festivities.

46 Gig Harbor, near Tacoma, a scenic fishing port that typifies the water-borne way of life along Puget Sound. Fishing has always been a mainstay of the Northwestern economy.

47 A former pioneer cabin, renovated as an information center, recalls the frontier heritage of America's Northwest—the last area of the continental United States to be settled.

48-49 Second Beach, Olympic Peninsula. The 900,000-acre Olympic National Park includes this protected seashore area, the pristine mountainous interior and several of the few rain forests outside the tropics.

50 Gem-like Lake Crescent, Olympic National Park.

51 Mountain goats thrive on the rocky heights of Mount Olympus and other nearby peaks.

52 Regal Mount Olympus, a fit home for the gods, towers 8000 feet above its wilderness setting.

53 Summit Ridge of Lightning Peak challenges the most experienced climbers in Olympic National Park, a mecca for mountaineers.

54-55 The 172 islands of the San Juan archipelago range in size from less than an acre to 134 acres and include four national parks. They are a favorite resort area.

56-57 The Hoh Valley Rain Forest grows luxuriantly in the peninsula's warm, wet climate.

BRITISH COLUMBIA

Coastal British Columbia is Canada's answer to California: it has an extensive and beautiful coastline, fertile lowlands, exciting cities and scenic mountains that protect the region from cold Arctic air. Mild winds from the Pacific help give it the warm climate that encourages outdoor life. Most British Columbians live in the Vancouver-Victoria region, in the province's southwestern corner. Mainland Vancouver is the larger city, but nearby Victoria, on Vancouver Island, is the capital of the province. Jewel-like green islands dot the waters between these busy ports, and their sheltered waterways carry goods and passengers all through the region.

Victoria welcomes its many visitors with a view of flowers along the Inner Harbour, where its impressive Parliament Buildings are outlined by colored lights at night. The Empress Hotel presides over this setting like the venerable queen whose name the city bears. Winding streets, trim gardens and tall red buses also recall Victoria's British heritage, while the setting sun on the provincial flag shows pride in the region's status as Canada's westernmost province. British Columbians have had to be independent and resourceful, like the pioneers of the American West. Until the Canadian Pacific Railroad finally reached Vancouver in 1887, the province was very much on its own, isolated by the mountains that made it so difficult to build roads and railroads to the coast. The enterprising spirit of those days is still manifested here, and the region's civic and cultural life has benefited from multi-racial contributions. Indians, Americans, Scandinavians, French, Dutch and Asians—all have made their mark on the area's way of life. One could spend weeks exploring Victoria and 285-mile-long Vancouver Island, but the claims of municipal Vancouver, across the water, are compelling in their own right.

Imposing mountains and quiet coastal scenes greet the eye from every vantage point in Vancouver. Queen Elizabeth Park, on 'Little Mountain,' has acres of winding paths through manicured grounds that overlook the whole city, as well as North Vancouver, across Burrand Inlet. Downtown, popular Stanley Park has an extensive acreage that includes two lakes, an open-air concert hall and the Royal Vancouver Yacht Club, where luxurious craft from international ports of call ride serenely at anchor. Horseshoe Bay is a busy point of departure for nearby recreation areas, including Vancouver Island. Here one can begin (or continue from Seattle) a tour of the Inside Passage, one of the world's most scenic water routes. Protected by a chain of coastal islands, the passage extends north to Prince Rupert, Juneau and other Alaskan ports. Luxurious cruise ships share this sea road with brawny freighters and sturdy tugs towing logs.

Along the way, numerous fjords reach deeply into the Coast Mountains, providing access to the less populous interior of British Columbia, where twentieth-century pioneers are still hewing their farms and settlements from the rolling country that extends to the Canadian Rockies. British Columbia's coat of arms carries a legend appropriate to this land. *Splendor Sine Occasu* : Splendor Without Diminishment.

59 British Columbia, Canada's only Pacific province, has the setting sun as its emblem.

64 Victoria's imposing Parliament Buildings can be seen by night long before one enters the Inner Harbour.

65 Butchart Gardens, considered by many the floral showplace of North America. Victoria's climate is so mild that flowers bloom almost year-round—one of the many ways in which the city reminds us of England.

60-61 Canada's maple-leaf flag, flanked by the colors of Great Britain and British Columbia, flies over Victoria, the provincial capital.

62-63 The historic Empress Hotel overlooks Victoria's busy Inner Harbour, the heart of the city.

66 The Coast Mountains loom over the British Columbian shoreline, separating the populous Victoria-Vancouver region from the more sparsely settled interior.

67 Vancouver Island's Pacific Undersea Gardens feature the world's only underwater theater— complete with scuba show and octopus.

68-69 Vancouver, 'Gem of the Pacific,' British Columbia's largest city. The Fraser River Gold Rush of 1858 brought people and prosperity to this formerly isolated coastal community.

70-71 Lights from the 1986 World Exposition in Vancouver reflect in the water at night.

*72 The prestigious Royal Vancouver Yacht Club,
as seen from Old Hastings Mill Park*

73 *Friends sip coffee and share a bench in
Vancouver with a cat.*

74-75 Waterfalls at Upper Arrow Lake exemplify the natural beauty that exerts its power over every visitor to British Columbia.

76 Light planes and snowmobiles provide modern mobility for the Eskimos of northern British Columbia.

77 Moonrise over the Canadian Pacific coast.

78 *A barn below Round Top Mountain, as fall color begins to appear.*

79 *A British Columbian forest of mingled evergreens and deciduous trees.*

COASTAL ALASKA

The coast of Alaska borders British Columbia and Yukon Territory until it swings west toward the remote Aleutian and Pribilof Islands, the first Alaskan territory discovered by Russian explorers who set out from Siberia in the eighteenth century. Access to this rugged region is mainly by sea and air, since road-building is difficult or impossible over much of the largest state.

Mountainous and forested, the coast of Alaska is mantled by glaciers, including those at awe-inspiring Glacier Bay, near the capital city of Juneau, and the vast Columbia Glacier on Prince William Sound, at the western edge of the coastal range that rims the Gulf of Alaska. Whales frequent these waters, which are also a rich fishing ground and the home of numerous colorful seabirds.

West of Prince William Sound, the Kenai Peninsula reaches south into the Gulf, forming sheltered Cook Inlet to the west. The peninsula is bordered on the east by the Kenai Mountains, on the west by sloping plains and shoreline communities, including Kenai, one of Alaska's oldest settlements. It began as a Russian trading post in 1791, after Vitus Bering, a Danish sea captian commissioned by Czar Peter the Great, had explored these waters and the sea named for him.

Literally millions of acres in the Alaskan Panhandle and southwest have been designated wildlife sanctuaries and national parklands, including Tongai National Forest, the largest on the continent. In these wilderness strongholds, such diverse species as the sea lion, brown bear, coastal fox and boldly marked puffin, with its brilliant red and yellow beak, are protected against depredation.

Cook Inlet, named for English navigator James Cook, the Northwest's most important explorer, runs north to Anchorage, Alaska's youngest and largest city. A bustling business and financial center, Anchorage is still growing and proud of it. The discovery of oil offshore in the late 1950s brought a new kind of gold rush into the region, reminiscent of Klondike days.

Southwest of Anchorage, the Alaska Peninsula and the Aleutian Islands curve into the North Pacific, separating it from the Bering Sea. The sparsely inhabited islands extend southwest for over a thousand miles, forming what is known as 'the land of the smoky sea.' On the Alaska Peninsula, Katmai National Park surrounds the site of the great Novarupta Volcano eruption of 1912—a reminder that this land is, and probably always will be, largely untamed.

Tlingit and Aleut Indians, European explorers, Russian trappers and traders, gold rushers and pioneers: all have looked upon the immense grandeur of this coast with wonder. The wonder remains.

81 A yacht silhouetted by sunrise in Kachemak Bay, off Alaska's Kenai Peninsula.

82 A Kotzebue Indian family in holiday dress.
Alaska's hardy people combine Indian, Russian
and pioneer ancestry.

82

83 The spirit houses of this Athabascan Indian cemetery are ornamented by the crosses of Russian Orthodoxy.

84

84 Kodiak Island residents of Russian descent gather on the grounds of their church. The Island was once a major fur-trading center.

85 A tiny Siberian chapel offers a stopping place for the solitary prayer and meditation deeply valued by the Russian Orthodox tradition.

86 The huge Columbia Glacier is the largest of the great ice flows that descend to the shores of Prince William Sound.

87 Glacier Bay—called Thunder Bay by the Indians from the sound made by calving glaciers—is one of the great natural attractions of Alaska's Inside Passage.

88-89 Alaskan Brown Bears sun themselves
beside one of their many fishing streams.

90 Salmon fishermen on Prince William Sound
haul in a good catch.

91 Pacific salmon leave the sea to swim up
freshwater streams to their inland spawning
grounds.

92 Sea lions bask on the rocks of Kenai Fjords National Park, which offers them a protected breeding ground.

93 Black-legged Kittiwakes at their principal rook—St Paul, Pribilof Islands.

94-95 Anchorage, Alaska, the state's largest city, seen from Earthquake Park on a summer evening.

96 The Matanuska River meanders through the Chugach Mountains east of Anchorage.

97 The fertile Matanuska Valley was settled by farmers fleeing the Midwestern Dust Bowl in the middle 1930s. Now it produces half of Alaska's crops.

98-99 The fishing town of Homer occupies a spit of land extending into Kachemak Bay from the scenic Kenai Peninsula.

100-101 Kachemak Bay State Park, with Poot Peak in the foreground backed by the glacial Kenai Mountains.

THE CASCADES AND THE COLUMBIA RIVER BASIN

The Cascade Range extends through the Northwest for over 700 miles, from southern British Columbia into northern California. From the North, the major volcanic cones are Baker, Glacier Peak, Rainier—the highest, at 14,400 feet—St Helens, Adams, Hood, Jefferson, the Three Sisters, Shasta and Lassen. Lesser peaks, also crowned by ice and snow, comprise the rest of the range, which is broken by crags, cliffs and deep canyons, notably the great Columbia River Gorge, a thoroughfare for Northwestern settlers. Only the Columbia was able to cut its way through the great natural barrier formed by these mountains.

Throughout the Cascade Range, much of which is preserved as national-park and wilderness land, streams plunge from steep cliffs and hundreds of lakes in glacial valleys mirror the beauty around them. Western hemlock, spruce and pine form an evergreen pedestal for the soaring white peaks.

The Columbia River, the West's major waterway, drains an area of 259,000 square miles from its source in the Canadian Rockies to the Columbia River Bar, west of Portland, where it surges into the Pacific. Its many tributaries include the Snake, the Okanogan, the Kootenay and the Willamette Rivers, and its basin has over one-third of the potential water power of the United States, now channeled for man's use by extensive hydroelectric projects that include canals and locks to maintain the river's navigability. Small vessels can bypass power dams on the lower Columbia and sail up the Snake River to the Idaho border.

The Columbia itself forms the boundary line between Washington and Oregon, from a point below its confluence with the Snake west to the Pacific. The city of Portland grew up near its juncture with the Willamette and became a maritime center of major influence in the region. Populated originally by seaworthy New Englanders who resettled here, Portland has orderly, tree-shaded streets, block-sized parks and peerless rose gardens that recall its colonial heritage. At the same time, it has turned toward the future with an ever-growing investment in commerce and industry.

On its 1200-mile journey to the sea, the Columbia travels through flowering orchards, quiet farmlands and wheat fields, and the unspoiled vistas of the Cascade Range with its waterfalls and wildflower meadows. Fishing ports and villages dot its banks and major highways parallel its course. The Mississippi of the West affords a unique perspective from which to view every aspect of the beautiful Pacific Northwest.

103 Mount Shuksan, Cascade Range, from Highwood Lake in Washington State.

104-105 *The swift-flowing Columbia River and its tributaries have cut innumerable canyons and gorges through Washington and Oregon.*

106-107 *Wizard's Island, in Oregon's Crater Lake—an island formed of volcanic debris. Here water gradually filled the basin of a collapsed volcano.*

108 *The Columbia River flows past Crown Point in the 60-mile-long gorge that forms the principal natural gap through the Cascades. Northwestern settlers floated their covered wagons downstream on rafts at this atypically placid section of the river.*

109 *Reeds along the Blitzen River in the Malheur National Wildlife Refuge, Oregon.*

110-111 Daisies, true chamomile and corn poppies form a wildflower mosaic in the Cascades.

112-113 A well-kept ranch in central Oregon's Crook County on an August morning.

114 *The Snoqualmie River plunges 270 feet at Snoqualmie Falls, east of Seattle, in its headlong descent to the Snohomish.*

115 *The wheat-bearing Palouse country of eastern Washington and Oregon takes its name from the Indian tribe.*

116-117 *Mount St Helens, Washington, after the devastating eruption of 1980, which laid waste to the countryside for over 100 miles around.*

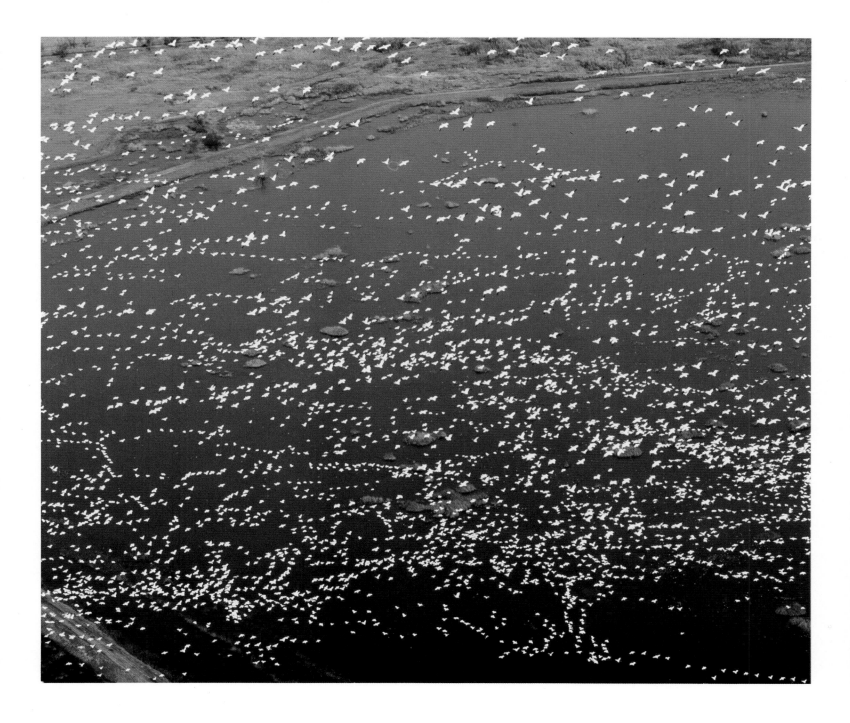

118 A chilly view of Mount Baker in the northern
part of Washington's Cascades.

119 Migratory snow geese on the Pacific flyway.

120 Grand Coulee Dam has turned the once-barren Columbia River Basin into half a million acres of productive farmland with a vast network of canals and reservoirs.

121 Bonneville Dam, 40 miles east of Portland, is another link in the chain of 11 dams that harness the Columbia River for human needs—power, irrigation and transport.

122 The Willamette River winds through Portland, Oregon, dividing the city's gracious residential area from the high-rise buildings of downtown's commercial center.

123 Portland's progressive Koin Tower reflects the city's dynamic growth in recent years. The friendly rivalry between Portland and Seattle, the urban centers of the US Northwest, is long-standing. Portlanders point out that theirs was an established city when Seattle was a rough camp on Puget Sound. Seattle residents respond—undeniably—that their Mount Rainier is higher than Mount Hood.

124-125 One of the Cascades' most beautiful peaks, Mount Hood, clothed in freshly fallen snow.